SAVINGS TRACKER

SAVING FOR :

SAVING GOAL :

STARTING BALANCE :

DATE	WITHDRAWAL	DEPOSIT	BALANCE	NOTES
DATE	WITHDRAWAL	DEPOSIT	BALANCE	NOTES

SAVINGS TRACKER

SAVING FOR :				
SAVING GOAL :		**STARTING BALANCE :**		

DATE	WITHDRAWAL	DEPOSIT	BALANCE	NOTES

SAVINGS TRACKER

SAVING FOR :				
SAVING GOAL :		STARTING BALANCE :		
DATE	WITHDRAWAL	DEPOSIT	BALANCE	NOTES

SAVINGS TRACKER

SAVING FOR :

SAVING GOAL : **STARTING BALANCE :**

DATE	WITHDRAWAL	DEPOSIT	BALANCE	NOTES

SAVINGS TRACKER

SAVING FOR :				
SAVING GOAL :		STARTING BALANCE :		
DATE	WITHDRAWAL	DEPOSIT	BALANCE	NOTES

SAVINGS TRACKER

SAVING FOR :				
SAVING GOAL :		STARTING BALANCE :		
DATE	WITHDRAWAL	DEPOSIT	BALANCE	NOTES

SAVINGS TRACKER

SAVING FOR :				
SAVING GOAL :		**STARTING BALANCE :**		
DATE	WITHDRAWAL	DEPOSIT	BALANCE	NOTES
DATE	WITHDRAWAL	DEPOSIT	BALANCE	NOTES

SAVINGS TRACKER

SAVING FOR :				
SAVING GOAL :		STARTING BALANCE :		
DATE	WITHDRAWAL	DEPOSIT	BALANCE	NOTES

SAVINGS TRACKER

SAVING FOR :				
SAVING GOAL :		**STARTING BALANCE :**		
DATE	**WITHDRAWAL**	**DEPOSIT**	**BALANCE**	**NOTES**

SAVINGS TRACKER

SAVING FOR :				
SAVING GOAL :		**STARTING BALANCE :**		
DATE	WITHDRAWAL	DEPOSIT	BALANCE	NOTES

SAVINGS TRACKER

SAVING FOR :				
SAVING GOAL :		STARTING BALANCE :		
DATE	WITHDRAWAL	DEPOSIT	BALANCE	NOTES

SAVINGS TRACKER

SAVING FOR :

SAVING GOAL :

STARTING BALANCE :

DATE	WITHDRAWAL	DEPOSIT	BALANCE	NOTES

SAVINGS TRACKER

SAVING FOR :

SAVING GOAL :   **STARTING BALANCE :**

DATE	WITHDRAWAL	DEPOSIT	BALANCE	NOTES
DATE	WITHDRAWAL	DEPOSIT	BALANCE	NOTES

SAVINGS TRACKER

SAVING FOR :

SAVING GOAL :

STARTING BALANCE :

DATE	WITHDRAWAL	DEPOSIT	BALANCE	NOTES

SAVINGS TRACKER

SAVING FOR :

SAVING GOAL : **STARTING BALANCE :**

DATE	WITHDRAWAL	DEPOSIT	BALANCE	NOTES

SAVING GOAL

DATE	WITHDRAWAL	DEPOSIT	BALANCE	NOTES

SAVINGS TRACKER

SAVING FOR :				
SAVING GOAL :		STARTING BALANCE :		
DATE	WITHDRAWAL	DEPOSIT	BALANCE	NOTES
DATE	WITHDRAWAL	DEPOSIT	BALANCE	NOTES

SAVINGS TRACKER

SAVING FOR :

SAVING GOAL :		STARTING BALANCE :		
DATE	WITHDRAWAL	DEPOSIT	BALANCE	NOTES
DATE	WITHDRAWAL	DEPOSIT	BALANCE	NOTES

SAVINGS TRACKER

SAVING FOR :				
SAVING GOAL :		**STARTING BALANCE :**		
DATE	WITHDRAWAL	DEPOSIT	BALANCE	NOTES

SAVINGS TRACKER

SAVING FOR :				
SAVING GOAL :		STARTING BALANCE :		
DATE	WITHDRAWAL	DEPOSIT	BALANCE	NOTES

SAVINGS TRACKER

SAVING FOR :

SAVING GOAL :   **STARTING BALANCE :**

DATE	WITHDRAWAL	DEPOSIT	BALANCE	NOTES

SAVINGS TRACKER

SAVING FOR :				
SAVING GOAL :		**STARTING BALANCE :**		
DATE	WITHDRAWAL	DEPOSIT	BALANCE	NOTES

SAVINGS TRACKER

SAVING FOR :

SAVING GOAL :   **STARTING BALANCE :**

DATE	WITHDRAWAL	DEPOSIT	BALANCE	NOTES

SAVINGS TRACKER

SAVING FOR :				
SAVING GOAL :		STARTING BALANCE :		
DATE	WITHDRAWAL	DEPOSIT	BALANCE	NOTES

SAVINGS TRACKER

SAVING FOR :				
SAVING GOAL :		STARTING BALANCE :		
DATE	WITHDRAWAL	DEPOSIT	BALANCE	NOTES
DATE	WITHDRAWAL	DEPOSIT	BALANCE	NOTES

SAVINGS TRACKER

SAVING FOR :				
SAVING GOAL :		STARTING BALANCE :		
DATE	WITHDRAWAL	DEPOSIT	BALANCE	NOTES
SAVING GOAL :				
DATE	WITHDRAWAL	DEPOSIT	BALANCE	NOTES

SAVINGS TRACKER

SAVING FOR :				
SAVING GOAL :		**STARTING BALANCE :**		
DATE	WITHDRAWAL	DEPOSIT	BALANCE	NOTES

SAVINGS TRACKER

SAVING FOR :				
SAVING GOAL :		**STARTING BALANCE :**		

DATE	WITHDRAWAL	DEPOSIT	BALANCE	NOTES

SAVINGS TRACKER

SAVING FOR :				
SAVING GOAL :		STARTING BALANCE :		
DATE	WITHDRAWAL	DEPOSIT	BALANCE	NOTES

SAVINGS TRACKER

SAVING FOR :				
SAVING GOAL :		**STARTING BALANCE :**		
DATE	WITHDRAWAL	DEPOSIT	BALANCE	NOTES
SAVING GOAL :		**DEPOSIT**	**BALANCE**	**NOTES**

SAVINGS TRACKER

SAVING FOR :				
SAVING GOAL :		STARTING BALANCE :		
DATE	WITHDRAWAL	DEPOSIT	BALANCE	NOTES

SAVINGS TRACKER

SAVING FOR :

SAVING GOAL : | **STARTING BALANCE :**

DATE	WITHDRAWAL	DEPOSIT	BALANCE	NOTES

SAVINGS TRACKER

SAVING FOR :				
SAVING GOAL :		**STARTING BALANCE :**		
DATE	WITHDRAWAL	DEPOSIT	BALANCE	NOTES

SAVINGS TRACKER

SAVING FOR :				
SAVING GOAL :		**STARTING BALANCE :**		
DATE	WITHDRAWAL	DEPOSIT	BALANCE	NOTES

SAVINGS TRACKER

SAVING FOR :				
SAVING GOAL :		**STARTING BALANCE :**		
DATE	WITHDRAWAL	DEPOSIT	BALANCE	NOTES

SAVINGS TRACKER

SAVING FOR :				
SAVING GOAL :		**STARTING BALANCE :**		
DATE	WITHDRAWAL	DEPOSIT	BALANCE	NOTES

SAVINGS TRACKER

SAVING FOR :				
SAVING GOAL :		**STARTING BALANCE :**		
DATE	WITHDRAWAL	DEPOSIT	BALANCE	NOTES
DATE	WITHDRAWAL	DEPOSIT	BALANCE	NOTES

SAVINGS TRACKER

SAVING FOR :				
SAVING GOAL :		**STARTING BALANCE :**		
DATE	WITHDRAWAL	DEPOSIT	BALANCE	NOTES

SAVINGS TRACKER

SAVING FOR :				
SAVING GOAL :		**STARTING BALANCE :**		
DATE	WITHDRAWAL	DEPOSIT	BALANCE	NOTES

SAVINGS TRACKER

SAVING FOR :				
SAVING GOAL :		STARTING BALANCE :		
DATE	WITHDRAWAL	DEPOSIT	BALANCE	NOTES

SAVINGS TRACKER

SAVING FOR :				
SAVING GOAL :		**STARTING BALANCE :**		
DATE	WITHDRAWAL	DEPOSIT	BALANCE	NOTES

SAVINGS TRACKER

SAVING FOR :

SAVING GOAL : | **STARTING BALANCE :**

DATE	WITHDRAWAL	DEPOSIT	BALANCE	NOTES

SAVINGS TRACKER

SAVING FOR :				
SAVING GOAL :		STARTING BALANCE :		
DATE	WITHDRAWAL	DEPOSIT	BALANCE	NOTES

SAVINGS TRACKER

SAVING FOR :

SAVING GOAL : | **STARTING BALANCE :**

DATE	WITHDRAWAL	DEPOSIT	BALANCE	NOTES

SAVINGS TRACKER

SAVING FOR :				
SAVING GOAL :		STARTING BALANCE :		

DATE	WITHDRAWAL	DEPOSIT	BALANCE	NOTES

SAVINGS TRACKER

SAVING FOR :				
SAVING GOAL :		STARTING BALANCE :		
DATE	WITHDRAWAL	DEPOSIT	BALANCE	NOTES

SAVINGS TRACKER

SAVING FOR :				
SAVING GOAL :		STARTING BALANCE :		
DATE	WITHDRAWAL	DEPOSIT	BALANCE	NOTES

SAVINGS TRACKER

SAVING FOR :				
SAVING GOAL :		STARTING BALANCE :		
DATE	WITHDRAWAL	DEPOSIT	BALANCE	NOTES

SAVINGS TRACKER

SAVING FOR :				
SAVING GOAL :		STARTING BALANCE :		
DATE	WITHDRAWAL	DEPOSIT	BALANCE	NOTES

SAVINGS TRACKER

SAVING FOR :				
SAVING GOAL :		**STARTING BALANCE :**		
DATE	WITHDRAWAL	DEPOSIT	BALANCE	NOTES

SAVINGS TRACKER

SAVING FOR :

SAVING GOAL :   **STARTING BALANCE :**

DATE	WITHDRAWAL	DEPOSIT	BALANCE	NOTES

SAVINGS TRACKER

SAVING FOR :				
SAVING GOAL :		**STARTING BALANCE :**		
DATE	WITHDRAWAL	DEPOSIT	BALANCE	NOTES

SAVINGS TRACKER

SAVING FOR :

SAVING GOAL : | **STARTING BALANCE :**

DATE	WITHDRAWAL	DEPOSIT	BALANCE	NOTES

SAVINGS TRACKER

SAVING FOR :

SAVING GOAL :		STARTING BALANCE :		
DATE	WITHDRAWAL	DEPOSIT	BALANCE	NOTES

SAVINGS TRACKER

SAVING FOR :				
SAVING GOAL :		STARTING BALANCE :		
DATE	WITHDRAWAL	DEPOSIT	BALANCE	NOTES

SAVINGS TRACKER

SAVING FOR :				
SAVING GOAL :		**STARTING BALANCE :**		
DATE	WITHDRAWAL	DEPOSIT	BALANCE	NOTES

SAVINGS TRACKER

SAVING FOR :				
SAVING GOAL :		**STARTING BALANCE :**		

DATE	WITHDRAWAL	DEPOSIT	BALANCE	NOTES

SAVINGS TRACKER

SAVING FOR :				
SAVING GOAL :		STARTING BALANCE :		
DATE	WITHDRAWAL	DEPOSIT	BALANCE	NOTES

SAVINGS TRACKER

SAVING FOR :				
SAVING GOAL :		STARTING BALANCE :		
DATE	WITHDRAWAL	DEPOSIT	BALANCE	NOTES

SAVINGS TRACKER

SAVING FOR :				
SAVING GOAL :		**STARTING BALANCE :**		
DATE	**WITHDRAWAL**	**DEPOSIT**	**BALANCE**	**NOTES**

SAVINGS TRACKER

SAVING FOR :				
SAVING GOAL :		**STARTING BALANCE :**		
DATE	WITHDRAWAL	DEPOSIT	BALANCE	NOTES

SAVINGS TRACKER

SAVING FOR :				
SAVING GOAL :		**STARTING BALANCE :**		
DATE	WITHDRAWAL	DEPOSIT	BALANCE	NOTES

SAVINGS TRACKER

SAVING FOR :				
SAVING GOAL :		**STARTING BALANCE :**		
DATE	WITHDRAWAL	DEPOSIT	BALANCE	NOTES

SAVINGS TRACKER

SAVING FOR :				
SAVING GOAL :		STARTING BALANCE :		
DATE	WITHDRAWAL	DEPOSIT	BALANCE	NOTES

SAVINGS TRACKER

SAVING FOR :				
SAVING GOAL :		**STARTING BALANCE :**		
DATE	WITHDRAWAL	DEPOSIT	BALANCE	NOTES
DATE	WITHDRAWAL	DEPOSIT	BALANCE	NOTES

SAVINGS TRACKER

SAVING FOR :

SAVING GOAL :   **STARTING BALANCE :**

DATE	WITHDRAWAL	DEPOSIT	BALANCE	NOTES

SAVINGS TRACKER

SAVING FOR :				
SAVING GOAL :		STARTING BALANCE :		
DATE	WITHDRAWAL	DEPOSIT	BALANCE	NOTES

SAVINGS TRACKER

SAVING FOR :				
SAVING GOAL :		STARTING BALANCE :		
DATE	WITHDRAWAL	DEPOSIT	BALANCE	NOTES

SAVINGS TRACKER

SAVING FOR :				
SAVING GOAL :		STARTING BALANCE :		
DATE	WITHDRAWAL	DEPOSIT	BALANCE	NOTES

SAVINGS TRACKER

SAVING FOR :				
SAVING GOAL :		STARTING BALANCE :		
DATE	WITHDRAWAL	DEPOSIT	BALANCE	NOTES

SAVINGS TRACKER

SAVING FOR :				
SAVING GOAL :		STARTING BALANCE :		
DATE	WITHDRAWAL	DEPOSIT	BALANCE	NOTES

SAVINGS TRACKER

SAVING FOR :				
SAVING GOAL :		**STARTING BALANCE :**		
DATE	WITHDRAWAL	DEPOSIT	BALANCE	NOTES
DATE	WITHDRAWAL	DEPOSIT	BALANCE	NOTES

SAVINGS TRACKER

SAVING FOR :				
SAVING GOAL :		**STARTING BALANCE :**		
DATE	WITHDRAWAL	DEPOSIT	BALANCE	NOTES

SAVINGS TRACKER

SAVING FOR :				
SAVING GOAL :		STARTING BALANCE :		

DATE	WITHDRAWAL	DEPOSIT	BALANCE	NOTES

SAVINGS TRACKER

SAVING FOR :

SAVING GOAL :   **STARTING BALANCE :**

DATE	WITHDRAWAL	DEPOSIT	BALANCE	NOTES

SAVINGS TRACKER

SAVING FOR :				
SAVING GOAL :		**STARTING BALANCE :**		
DATE	WITHDRAWAL	DEPOSIT	BALANCE	NOTES

SAVINGS TRACKER

SAVING FOR :				
SAVING GOAL :		STARTING BALANCE :		
DATE	WITHDRAWAL	DEPOSIT	BALANCE	NOTES
DATE	WITHDRAWAL	DEPOSIT	BALANCE	NOTES

SAVINGS TRACKER

SAVING FOR :				
SAVING GOAL :		STARTING BALANCE :		
DATE	WITHDRAWAL	DEPOSIT	BALANCE	NOTES

SAVINGS TRACKER

SAVING FOR :				
SAVING GOAL :		**STARTING BALANCE :**		
DATE	WITHDRAWAL	DEPOSIT	BALANCE	NOTES

SAVINGS TRACKER

SAVING FOR :				
SAVING GOAL :		STARTING BALANCE :		
DATE	WITHDRAWAL	DEPOSIT	BALANCE	NOTES

SAVINGS TRACKER

SAVING FOR :

SAVING GOAL :

STARTING BALANCE :

DATE	WITHDRAWAL	DEPOSIT	BALANCE	NOTES

SAVINGS TRACKER

SAVING FOR :				
SAVING GOAL :		STARTING BALANCE :		
DATE	**WITHDRAWAL**	**DEPOSIT**	**BALANCE**	**NOTES**

SAVINGS TRACKER

SAVING FOR :				
SAVING GOAL :		**STARTING BALANCE :**		
DATE	WITHDRAWAL	DEPOSIT	BALANCE	NOTES

SAVINGS TRACKER

SAVING FOR :				
SAVING GOAL :		**STARTING BALANCE :**		
DATE	**WITHDRAWAL**	**DEPOSIT**	**BALANCE**	**NOTES**

SAVINGS TRACKER

SAVING FOR :				
SAVING GOAL :		STARTING BALANCE :		
DATE	WITHDRAWAL	DEPOSIT	BALANCE	NOTES

SAVINGS TRACKER

SAVING FOR :

SAVING GOAL : | **STARTING BALANCE :**

DATE	WITHDRAWAL	DEPOSIT	BALANCE	NOTES

SAVINGS TRACKER

SAVING FOR :				
SAVING GOAL :		STARTING BALANCE :		
DATE	**WITHDRAWAL**	**DEPOSIT**	**BALANCE**	**NOTES**

SAVINGS TRACKER

SAVING FOR :				
SAVING GOAL :		STARTING BALANCE :		
DATE	WITHDRAWAL	DEPOSIT	BALANCE	NOTES

SAVINGS TRACKER

SAVING FOR :				
SAVING GOAL :		**STARTING BALANCE :**		
DATE	WITHDRAWAL	DEPOSIT	BALANCE	NOTES

SAVINGS TRACKER

SAVING FOR :				
SAVING GOAL :		STARTING BALANCE :		
DATE	WITHDRAWAL	DEPOSIT	BALANCE	NOTES

SAVINGS TRACKER

SAVING FOR :				
SAVING GOAL :		STARTING BALANCE :		
DATE	WITHDRAWAL	DEPOSIT	BALANCE	NOTES
DATE	WITHDRAWAL	DEPOSIT	BALANCE	NOTES

SAVINGS TRACKER

SAVING FOR :

SAVING GOAL : | **STARTING BALANCE :**

DATE	WITHDRAWAL	DEPOSIT	BALANCE	NOTES

SAVINGS TRACKER

SAVING FOR :				
SAVING GOAL :		**STARTING BALANCE :**		
DATE	WITHDRAWAL	DEPOSIT	BALANCE	NOTES

SAVINGS TRACKER

SAVING FOR :

SAVING GOAL : | **STARTING BALANCE :**

DATE	WITHDRAWAL	DEPOSIT	BALANCE	NOTES

SAVINGS TRACKER

| SAVING FOR : | | | | |
| SAVING GOAL : | | STARTING BALANCE : | | |

DATE	WITHDRAWAL	DEPOSIT	BALANCE	NOTES

SAVINGS TRACKER

SAVING FOR :				
SAVING GOAL :		STARTING BALANCE :		
DATE	WITHDRAWAL	DEPOSIT	BALANCE	NOTES

SAVINGS TRACKER

SAVING FOR :				
SAVING GOAL :		STARTING BALANCE :		
DATE	WITHDRAWAL	DEPOSIT	BALANCE	NOTES

SAVINGS TRACKER

SAVING FOR :

SAVING GOAL :   **STARTING BALANCE :**

DATE	WITHDRAWAL	DEPOSIT	BALANCE	NOTES

SAVINGS TRACKER

SAVING FOR :				
SAVING GOAL :		STARTING BALANCE :		
DATE	WITHDRAWAL	DEPOSIT	BALANCE	NOTES

SAVINGS TRACKER

SAVING FOR :

SAVING GOAL : | **STARTING BALANCE :**

DATE	WITHDRAWAL	DEPOSIT	BALANCE	NOTES

SAVINGS TRACKER

SAVING FOR :

SAVING GOAL : **STARTING BALANCE :**

DATE	WITHDRAWAL	DEPOSIT	BALANCE	NOTES

SAVINGS TRACKER

SAVING FOR :				
SAVING GOAL :		STARTING BALANCE :		
DATE	WITHDRAWAL	DEPOSIT	BALANCE	NOTES

SAVINGS TRACKER

SAVING FOR :				
SAVING GOAL :		**STARTING BALANCE :**		
DATE	WITHDRAWAL	DEPOSIT	BALANCE	NOTES

SAVINGS TRACKER

SAVING FOR :				
SAVING GOAL :		STARTING BALANCE :		
DATE	WITHDRAWAL	DEPOSIT	BALANCE	NOTES

SAVINGS TRACKER

SAVING FOR :				
SAVING GOAL :		**STARTING BALANCE :**		
DATE	WITHDRAWAL	DEPOSIT	BALANCE	NOTES

SAVINGS TRACKER

SAVING FOR :				
SAVING GOAL :		STARTING BALANCE :		
DATE	WITHDRAWAL	DEPOSIT	BALANCE	NOTES

SAVINGS TRACKER

SAVING FOR :				
SAVING GOAL :		STARTING BALANCE :		
DATE	WITHDRAWAL	DEPOSIT	BALANCE	NOTES

SAVINGS TRACKER

SAVING FOR :				
SAVING GOAL :		**STARTING BALANCE :**		
DATE	**WITHDRAWAL**	**DEPOSIT**	**BALANCE**	**NOTES**

SAVINGS TRACKER

SAVING FOR :				
SAVING GOAL :		STARTING BALANCE :		
DATE	WITHDRAWAL	DEPOSIT	BALANCE	NOTES

SAVINGS TRACKER

SAVING FOR :

SAVING GOAL : | **STARTING BALANCE :**

DATE	WITHDRAWAL	DEPOSIT	BALANCE	NOTES

SAVINGS TRACKER

SAVING FOR :

SAVING GOAL :		STARTING BALANCE :		
DATE	WITHDRAWAL	DEPOSIT	BALANCE	NOTES

www.ingramcontent.com/pod-product-compliance
Lightning Source LLC
Chambersburg PA
CBHW071351150726
47997CB00002B/942